P9-DMS-306

PITA-TEN

Volume 1

by
Koge-Donbo

CRETE PUBLIC LIBRARY
1177 N. MAIN
CRETE, IL 60417
708/672-8017

Los Angeles • Tokyo • London

ANGA
GE-DONBO

Translator - Nan Rymer
English Adaptation - Adam Arnold
Copy Editor - Tim Beedle
Retouch and Lettering - Jennifer Nunn
Cover Layout - Raymond Makowski
Graphic Designer - James Lee

Editor - Paul Morrissey
Managing Editor - Jill Freshney
Production Coordinator - Antonio DePietro
Production Manager - Jennifer Miller & Mutsumi Miyazaki
Art Director - Matt Alford
Editorial Director - Jeremy Ross
VP of Production - Ron Klamert
President & C.O.O. - John Parker
Publisher & C.E.O. - Stuart Levy

Email: editor@TOKYOPOP.com

Come visit us online at www.TOKYOPOP.com

A TOKYOPOP® Manga

TOKYOPOP Inc.
5900 Wilshire Blvd. Suite 2000
Los Angeles, CA 90036

Pita-Ten Vol. 1

©2000 Koge-Donbo.
First published in Japan in 2000 by Media Works Inc., Tokyo, Japan.
English publication rights arranged through Media Works Inc.

English text copyright ©2004 TOKYOPOP Inc.

All rights reserved. No portion of this book may be reproduced or transmitted in any form or by any means without written permission from the copyright holders. This manga is a work of fiction. Any resemblance to actual events or locales or persons, living or dead, is entirely coincidental.

ISBN: 1-59182-627-6

First TOKYOPOP printing: January 2004

10 9 8 7 6

Printed in the USA

Contents

Lesson 1

How to Acquaint Oneself With a Neighbor

MORNINGS ARE ALWAYS A PAIN.
LET'S SEE. STOVE IS OFF...CHECK.
BURNABLE GARBAGE... CHECK.
HOUSE LOCKED UP...
CHECK.
EVERY DAY IT'S THE SAME OLD THING.
....
I'M HEADING OUT.
NOTHING EVER CHANGES.
GOOD MORNING... SU!!
OH, GOOD MOR–

PLEASE GO OUT WITH ME!!

PLEASE...
DON'T RUN!

WELL, THAT WAS CERTAINLY INTERESTING.
HEY! KOTAROU-CHAN!
KO-TAROU-CHAN!
WHAT THE HECK WAS THAT ALL ABOUT?
AND WHO ON EARTH WAS THAT PERSON?!
OH.
KOTAROU-CHAN!!!

GEE WHIZ, KOTAROU-CHAN! I CALLED YOUR NAME LIKE A BAZILLION TIMES!
OOPS.
SORRY, KOBOSHI-CHAN.
SHEESH! YOU'VE GOTTA BE MORE ATTENTIVE!
YOU CAN'T BE DAYDREAMING WITH MIDDLE SCHOOL ENTRANCE EXAMS COMING UP!
SO, DID YOU FINISH YESTERDAY'S DICTATION ASSIGNMENT?!
OR HOW ABOUT THE GEOGRAPHY HOMEWORK?!
HEY, ARE YOU EVEN LISTENING TO ME ANYMORE?!
YEP.
ALL DONE.

OH, AND HERE.
MATH
22 Lines
CHECK YOUR MATH HOMEWORK.
YOU'VE GOT BOARD DUTY TODAY, RIGHT?
AHH-
RRRAAWWRR!! I'M SOOO... STOKED!!
Yes, I'm being sarcastic!
HUH? HEADING HOME ALREADY?
YEAH, SEE YA.
YOU'RE MISHA-SAN, RIGHT?
YES, MA'AM!
YOUR TEST RESULTS WERE STUNNING. I'M SURE YOU'LL DO FINE HERE.
TEE HEE HEE. THANK YOU VERY MUCH, MA'AM.
BUT STARTING TOMORROW, WEAR A UNIFORM. THAT OUTFIT'S A BIT... ORNATE.

どさ
DROP
ぱさ
RUSTLE

くるっ
HMM? FRIEND OF YOURS, MISHA-SAN??
BIT SHY, ISN'T HE?
CAN'T PLACE HIM THOUGH.
THE KEY TO CONQUERING YOUR EXAMS... IS YOUR HEALTH!
YOU GET SICK NOW, AND IT'S OVER! BUT THAT'S NOT THE ONLY THING!

YOU HAVE TO STUDY UNTIL YOU DROP!
"THERE IS NO ROYAL ROAD IN GEOMETRY!"
EUCLID SAID THAT, AND THE SAME'S TRUE FOR LEARNING! EH?
!
つかつか
WHA-WHAT THE?
ぴたっ。
Hello!

YOU KNOW HER, HIGUCHI?
N-NO, SIR. I—
LOOK, I DON'T KNOW WHAT THIS IS ALL ABOUT, BUT WHY DON'T YOU SAVE IT UNTIL AFTER REVIEW?
NOW, WHY DON'T YOU COME TO THE BOARD AND SOLVE NUMBER 67 FOR US.
....
HOW EMBARRASSING.
FLEE FLEE
WHAT'S SHE WANT FROM ME?
BUT PLEASE KEEP YOUR GIRLFRIENDS OUT OF MY CLASS.
GOOD.
WHO THE HECK IS SHE?
OH WELL. WHATEVER... AT LEAST SHE'S GONE NOW...

WELCOME HOOOOOOME!! TEE HEE HEE!

SLAM
BONK!!
GYAH!!
BIG MEANIE!
IS...IS THIS REALLY HAPPENING?
MY HEAD!
...?...

UGHHH!
OWWIE OWW OWW OUCH.
......
TEE HEE HEE HEE!! HI-HI-HIYA-SU!!
I'M YER NEW NEIGHBOR! JUST MOVED IN TODAY.
NAME'S MISHA!

NICE TA MEET CHAAA!
WHA?!
TEE HEE HEE.
SOWWY FOR ALL THE TWOUBLE.
YEP, I'M OKIE DOKIE DANDY WANDY-SU.
SO THIS MORNING, THAT WAS A *GREETING?*
YES-SIREE!
SAY, YOU ALWAYS CARRY ONE OF THOSE STICKIE THINGYS AROUND?
NO...NOT *ALL* THE TIME.
OHHH. I SEE.
GUESS I'VE STILL GOT A TON OF GETTIN' USED TO!
TEE HEE HEE HEE!
......?
MISHA VERY, VERY SOWWY FOR ALL THE TROUBLE.
YOUR KINDNESS JUST WARMS MY HEART! YOU'RE SUCH A WONDERFUL PERSON.

I'M GLAD YOU'RE FEELING BETTER MISS, URR–
OOH!
IT'S MISHA! TEE HEE!
I'LL BE LIVIN' RIGHT NEXT DOOR TO YA! EVEN GOIN' TO THE SAME SCHOOL!
I'M PLEASED TO MAKE YOUR ACQUAIN-TANCE.
HOW VERY... POLITE. MY NAME'S KOTAROU HIGUCHI.
NICE TO MEET YOU...I GUESS.
BUT WOW, THIS IS EXCITIN'! FIRST TIME AWAY FROM MOMMA. GUESS I'M JUST A REGULAR WORKIN' GIRL NOW, HUH?

NOT TO BE RUDE, BUT I NEED TO GET DINNER STARTED.
WHOA, YOU MAKE YOUR OWN DINNER?! NEVER SEEN A KID DO THAT BEFORE!
OKAY, TIME FOR YOU TO GO–
BUT WHY? YOU LIKE TO COOK OR SOMETHIN'?
NO...MY MOM DIED.
SO, MY DAD AND I SPLIT THE CHORES.
I'M IN CHARGE OF COOKING AND CLEANING.
OH, THE *TRAGEDY* OF IT ALL!!
TO BE SO YOUNG, AND YET SO DOWN-TRODDEN!
I MUST SOMEHOW REPAY YOU FOR ALL THE TROUBLE I'VE CAUSED!!
AH HA! I'VE GOT IT! SU!!

HOW ABOUT I BECOME YOUR NEW MOMMA?!
SORRY, I'LL PASS.

ARGH!!
OWWIE OWW OWW OWW!!
......
CUT OURSELF AGAIN, DID WE?
FEEL FREE TO HELP YOURSELF TO THE BAND-AIDS.
TH-THANK YOU.
SORRY, BUT...KINDA NEVER DID THIS BEFORE. SU.
......
DON'T YOU THINK YOU'VE *HELPED* ENOUGH?
NO WAY!!
NO HOW!!
I'M GONNA DO IT! SU!!
......
ARG-GHH!!
YOU'RE THE ONE WHO WANTED TO HELP.
AHH SHUCKS.
JUST GIVE IT UP!
ARR-GH!!
NO WAY!
NAH UH!
I SAID I WAS GONNA COOK YOU SOMETHIN' YUMMY AND I SURE AIN'T GONNA GIVE UP 'TILL I WOWS YA!!
JUST YOU WAIT AND SEE, MISTER!! THAT'S A PWOMISE!!
......

IT'S... ALLLL...
...DONNNEEE!!
PRESENTING YOUR CURRY! SU!!
I DID IT! I TRULY-ULY DID IT!! I COOKED SOMETHIN'! YAHOO!!
UM, ALL YOU DID WAS BUTCHER SOME POTA-TOES...
THIS... THIS COULD CHANGE MY WHOLE LIFE!!
SO KOTAROU-KUN, WAS I OF GOOD USE TO YOU TODAY?
WELL...
...YOU KINDA HELPED. I SUPPOSE.
AWRIGHT! KOTAROU-KUN SAID I WAS USE-FUL!!
WELL THEN...

...SINCE YOU PROBABLY HAVE *OODLES* OF HOMEWORK...
...LOOKS LIKE I'LL BE TAKING MY LEAVE. TEE HEE!
UM, OKAY.
THANK YOU VERY MUCH FOR TODAY. DO TAKE CARE.
HEY, HOLD UP!

HMM?
IT'S FOR HELPING CUT THE POTATOES.

THANK YOU! SU!!
HMM, HOW'S THIS OPEN AGAIN?
OH, GOT IT. OKIES, WELL... THANKS AGAIN!
HUH? WAIT, ISN'T THE DOOR THAT WAY?
WE'RE ON THE THIRD FLOOR!
TEE HEE HEE! I KNOW, BUT I KINDA LOST MY KEY.
THAT'S NOT THE POINT.
DON'T YOU WORRY 'BOUT IT.
I MEAN...

...I AM AN ANGEL AFTER ALL.

WHAT ARE YOU, CRAZY?!
GET DOWN FROM THERE!!
IT ALL FELT LIKE PART OF A DREAM TO ME.
AND ALL I COULD THINK WAS, "WOW! DIDN'T KNOW THEY MADE DRESSES LIKE THAT."
THE POTATOES LOOK A LITTLE DIFFERENT TODAY.
Dad →
YEP, I KNOW.

カチャ
はっ
PLEASE GO OUT WITH ME!!
OH, I'LL GO OUT WITH YOU ALL RIGHT!!
BUT FIRST...
...YOU'LL HAVE TO DEFEAT ME!!
GOOD GRIP... CHECK.
SHE'S... SHE'S DEAD.

EVERY MORNING AT 8:23 ON THE DOT.
IN THIS VERY SPOT. OUTSIDE THESE VERY GATES.
I WAIT FOR HIM. JUST AS I HAVE...
...SO MANY DAYS PRIOR.
AT 8:26, LIKE CLOCK-WORK...
...I HEAR THOSE FAMILIAR SHUFFLES.
AND THINK TO MYSELF, "HE'S HERE!!"

Lesson 2
How to Properly Fight
An Older Woman
GOOD MOR-
GOOD MORNING! SU!!

......!
UH, AHH...
...G-G-GOOD MORNING.
UM, SORRY, BUT...
...I DON'T BELIEVE WE'VE MET.
YEAH, SHE'S MY NEW NEXT-DOOR NEIGHBOR.
NAME'S MISHA! TEE HEE!!
PLEASED TO MEET-CHA!!
......!
WELL, SINCE SHE IS ONE OF KOTAROU-CHAN'S' FRIENDS...
MY NAME'S KOBOSHI UEMATSU.
...THE LEAST I CAN DO IS BE NICE TO HER.
IT'S NICE TO MEET YOU ALSO.
SO MISHA-SAN, WHEN DID YOU MOVE HERE?

JUST FLEW IN YESTERDAY! WHEE!
......
......
THE MIDDLE SCHOOL'S OVER IN THAT BUILDING.
TEE HEE HEE. GOTCHA! SU!
WHAT JUST HAPPENED?!
WE'RE IN THIS ONE.
WHA-WHAT THE?!
OKIE DOKIE, SMOKIE.

WAIT. IF SHE'S IN MIDDLE SCHOOL, THEN THAT MAKES HER...
...AN OLDER WOMAN!!
JUST WHAT WAS ALL THAT BACK THERE?!
THEY WERE WAY TOO TOUCHY FEELY!!
HOW DARE SHE JUST DRAPE HERSELF...
...ALL OVER MY BELOVED KOTAROU-CHAN?! WHY HIM?!
WHAT ARE YOU DOING?
HUH?! AH, N-NOTHING!!
OH NO! SINCE THEY'RE NEIGHBORS...
THEY CAN VISIT AT ANY TIME!
は!!
IN SIX WHOLE YEARS, I'VE ONLY BEEN OVER FOUR TIMES!!
TAAAH-HHHH!!
GYYAAH!!

YOU LOUSY... HIT AND RUN... SCAM ARTIST YOU!!
ZIP IT, YOU UGL... ERR, LET'S DROP IT.
STILL, PHEW! DIDN'T THINK I'D MAKE IT FOR A SECOND THERE.
MORNIN', TEN-CHAN.
RIGHT AT THE BELL, DUDE.
JUST HOW I AM.
URGH!! THEY'RE ALL AGAINST ME!
I MIGHT NOT BE CUTE OR GROWN UP OR LIVE NEXT TO HIM.
BUT DARN IT!! I'VE BEEN HIS BIGGEST FAN FOR SIX WHOLE YEARS!
YOU HEAR THAT?!
I'VE GOT SENIORITY, DANG NABBIT!!
WHAT'S UP WITH HER?!
.....

AND I AM SURE NOT GOING TO LOSE TO THE LIKES OF HER!
IN ESTAB-LISHING A RECIPROCAL RELATION-SHIP...
...IF YOU INCREASE ONE SIDE OF THE EQUATION, THEN YOU MUST DO THE SAME...
HE HE HE.
OH, KOTAROU-CHAN ♡
IF THE AMOUNT OF WATER IS X DECI-LITERS...
ふ
NOW IF WE INCREASE THE VOLUME TWICE, THEN THE DEPTH OF Y...
!

WHA?!
WHAT THE HECK ARE YA DOIN', YA LOON?!
HEY, SIMMER DOWN BACK THERE, UEMATSU!
WHAT DO YOU THINK THIS IS, A BARN?!
B-BUT THERE'S SOMEONE OUT THERE.
THERE'S NOTHING OUT THERE, UEMATSU.
TEE HEE HEE HEE HEE!
GYAAHHH!!
TEE HEE HEE. JUST CHECKIN' UP ON KOTAROU-KUN.
W-WH-WHA-WHAT?!
WHOA, THIS JUNK'S PRETTY BORIN', HUH?
HELLO?! WE'RE IN THE MIDDLE OF CLASS HERE!!
NOW SCAT, YOU!!
THE NERVE OF SOME PEOP—
EWW, NOW SHE'S DONE IT! I BET HE'S GOING TO TELL HER OFF.
GO ON, KOTAROU-CHAN. YOU TELL HER GOOD!

す、
HERE.
DON'T YOU KNOW THAT'S DANGER-OUS?
THERE.
MUCH BETTER.
......
PLEASE HEAD BACK TO CLASS NOW, MISS.
TEE HEE HEE. SORRY FOR INTERRUPTIN'.

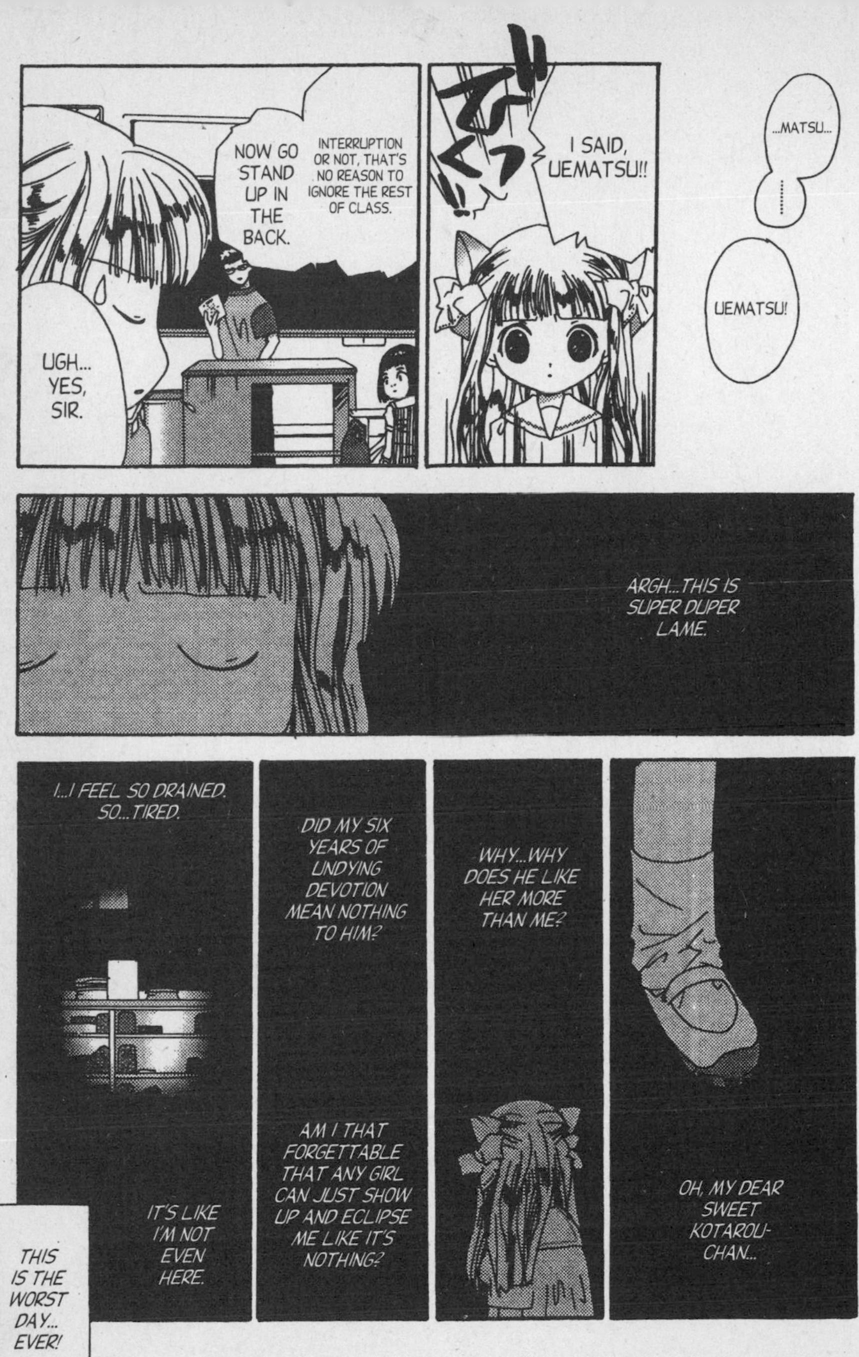
...MATSU... ......
UEMATSU!
I SAID, UEMATSU!!
INTERRUPTION OR NOT, THAT'S NO REASON TO IGNORE THE REST OF CLASS.
NOW GO STAND UP IN THE BACK.
UGH... YES, SIR.
ARGH...THIS IS SUPER DUPER LAME.
OH, MY DEAR SWEET KOTAROU-CHAN...
WHY...WHY DOES HE LIKE HER MORE THAN ME?
DID MY SIX YEARS OF UNDYING DEVOTION MEAN NOTHING TO HIM?
AM I THAT FORGETTABLE THAT ANY GIRL CAN JUST SHOW UP AND ECLIPSE ME LIKE IT'S NOTHING?
I...I FEEL SO DRAINED. SO...TIRED.
IT'S LIKE I'M NOT EVEN HERE.
THIS IS THE WORST DAY... EVER!

HUH?
JUST WHAT DO YOU THINK YOU'RE DOING, HIGUCHI?

I THINK I'LL STAND UP ALSO, SIR.
I SEE. WELL, SUIT YOURSELF.
NOW, WHERE WAS I?
......
......
I'M REALLY SORRY.
FOR WHAT?
UM...
... NOTHIN'!
?
KOTAROU-CHAN...
THAT'S IT!

I HAVE TO PROTECT KOTAROU-CHAN!

IT'S ALL YOU, KOTAROU!
GOTCHA!

WHA?!
KO...
...TA...
...ROU-
-KUN!!
LOOK OUT!!

KOTAROU-KUN!
CAREFUL!
UM, MISS?
FOR KOTAROU-KUN!
I NEED TO ASK YOU TO SIT THIS ONE OUT.

. . . .
......
UM, MISHA-SAN?
NOT TO BE RUDE...
...BUT DO YOU KNOW WHAT SOCCER IS?
HEE HEE HEE. KOTAROU-KUN... FUNNY.
YOU OKIES? SU?

HEY, LOOK OUT!!

KOTAROU-KUN!!
SUUU!
Splash
AT LEAST...
...IT'S ONLY YOUR GYM CLOTHES THAT GOT WET, RIGHT?
SO TELL ME, HOW'S IT FEEL TO GO COM-MANDO?
......
TEN-CHAN, PLEASE! DON'T BE CRUDE!!

YOO-HOO, KOTAROU-KUN!!
OVER HERE! TEE HEE HEE!
DIDN'T THINK YA HAD A REVIEW TODAY...
...SO I'VE BEEN WAITING FOR YOU!
YOU HAVE A TRACK-SUIT?
NAH, JUST BORROWING IT 'CAUSE I GOT WETTY WET. ♪
OHHH, SO YOU'RE GOING COMMANDO TOO?
YOU DIRTY OLD PERVERT!

YOU DIDN'T GET HURT TODAY, DID YA? SU?
UM, NAH. TH-THANKS.
OH YAH? *WELL*, THAT'S A GOODY GOOD THING DEN.
EWW, I ALMOST FORGOTS. I HAD A GOODY GOOD THING HAPPEN TO MEES TOO. ♡
REALLY ?

LOOKIE LOOKIE!! YOU KNOW THAT OUTFIT YOU WERE WEARIN'?!
WELL, NOW WEES MATCH!! YAY! ♪
HEY!!
植松
*UEMATSU
THOSE ARE MY GYM CLOTHES!!

(=_=)
Σ(￣□￣;)
(;´Д`)
HEY, WAY TO GO, MAN. YOU WENT THROUGH THE WHOLE DAY JUST TALKING IN "LETTER FACE." NICE.
NEXT MAHJONG LOSER HAS TO END EVERY-THING WITH "DATTCHA!" 'KAY?
HE USED "LETTER FACE" THIS WHOLE TIME?

Lesson 3

How to Perfect a Celebration

OKAY, LISTEN UP GOOD, KOTAROU-CHAN!
WHATEVER YOU DO TONIGHT, JUST MAKE SURE YOU EXERCISE ONLY THE MOST *EXTREME* CAUTION AROUND MISHA-SAN!! YOU GOT IT?!
......
UM... S-SURE.
UH, I WISH I COULD WALK YOU HOME, BUT... UM, I'VE GOT BALLET PRACTICE. AND, UH, MY PARENTS ARE MAKING ME GO. SO, I CAN'T GET OUTTA THAT. PLUS, YOU'VE GOT REVIEW...
AND AS MUCH AS I'M STRESSING ABOUT NOT BEING YOUR BODY GUARD–
THE TRAIN'S HERE, DORK.
GYAAH!! STOP IT, TEN-CHAN! HANDS OFF! LEGGO!!
......
Love ya, Kotarou-chan!! Bye bye!! Bye! Byyye!!

......
"EXTREME CAUTION"? FOR WHAT? OH, WAIT...HER.
TEE HEE HEE HEE HEE!
WELCOME BACK! SUUUU!! ♪
TEE HEE HEE! GUESS WHAT, KOTAROU-KUN?! GUESS WHAT!!
I WAS WAITIN' FOR YA'S THE WHOOOLE TIME! SU!
YOU WAS AT REVIEW TODAY, WEREN'TCHA? YEAH, I KNOW, I KNOW! DON'T WORRY. I DIDN'T FOLLOW YA THIS TIME! SU!
OKIES, UM...THE POINT IS...WELL, YOU SEE...
I...
SLAM

GEE, MY MOCK EXAM'S NEXT SUNDAY.
GUESS I BETTER GET CRACKING ON MY HOMEWORK.
LANGUAGE AND SOCIAL STUDIES FOR SCHOOL, AND A MATH WORK-SHEET FOR REVIEW.
SIGH.
......
ふ
NOW THEN...
...LET'S GET STARTED.

カリ
カリ
カリ
カリ
カリ
カリ
カリ
カリ
カリ
カリ
ギッ
カッ

......
I WAS KIND OF HOPING...
...THAT YOU'D PLEASE STOP THAT INCESSANT SCRATCHING.
YAY! YAHOO! KOTAROU-KUN FINALLY CAME OUT! YIPPIE!
UM, SO, UM...I HAVE SOMETHIN' TO BE TELLIN' YA! SU!!
LOOK, MISHA-SAN, I'M KIND OF TRYING TO STUDY.
I THINK YOU SHOULD SPEND SOME TIME AT HOME.
WELL, IF I GO HOME...
...THEN I WON'T GET TO SEE YOU ANYMORES AND I'D BE LONELY.

OH...I SEE. SORRY. I FORGOT YOU LIVED ALONE.
YEP YEP YEP. SU!!
UH, MISHA-SAN?
EWW! EWW! WHAT?!
SO, WHAT WAS IT YOU WANTED TO TELL ME?
BUT PLEASE, KEEP IT SHORT. I HAVE TO STUDY.
YESSIREE! ROGER. SU!!
WELL, YOU SEE...TEE HEE HEE!

I'M GONNAS HAVE A HOUSE PARTY! A MISHA'S MOVIN' IN BASH! AND YOU'RE INVITED!!! TEE HEE!
祝
祝
*Celebrate
NOT TO BE RUDE OR ANYTHING, BUT COULD WE DO THIS ANOTHER TIME?
I *REALLY* NEED TO GET BACK TO STUDYING!
AND DAT'S THE REASON WHY! SU!
はふ
はふ
THAT'S ALL FINE AND DANDY! *BUT WHY NOW OF ALL TIMES?!*

OKAY DOKEY! HOWS ABOUT RIGHT AFTER YA'S ALL DONE STUDYIN'?!
......
......
UM, IS DAT A NO GO? SU?
......
......
OH, ALL RIGHT.
LET ME FINISH THE MAJOR STUFF.
YAHOO!! PARTY PARTY PARTY!
HOWEVER!
WHEN I GET THERE I NEED TO TELL YOU SOMETHING, OKAY?
YESSIREE, BOB! GOTCHA. SU!
......
I'VE GOTTA LAY DOWN SOME GUIDELINES.

....
YAHOOO! KOTAROU-KUN'S HERE! SU!!
I'VE BEENS WAITIN' FOR YA!! YAY!
WHOA!!
!!
....

WELCOME TO MY HUMBLE ABODE.
......
TH- THANKS FOR INVITING ME.

UM, MISHA-SAN?
YO?
PLEASE TELL ME YOU DON'T ACTUALLY LIVE LIKE THIS.
YEAH, GUESS I'M A PACK RAT. HEE!
IT'S ACTUALLY KINDA FUN IF YOU GET USED TO IT! WHEE!
......
DO YOU EVEN HAVE A PLACE TO SLEEP IN THIS MESS, MISHA-SAN?!
HMMM? WHATCHA DOIN', KOTAROU-KUN?
IT'S CALLED CLEANING.
WHOAAA.
YOU MUST LIKE CLEANIN' STUFF. DON'TCHA, KOTAROU-KUN?
NO, I DON'T.
BUT FOR THIS PLACE, I'LL MAKE AN EXCEPTION.
I GUESS THINGS JUST END UP EVERY WHICH A WHERE.
IT'S NOTHING LIKE THIS OVER THERE. SU.
......
WHA? "OVER THERE"?
YOU USED TO LIVE OVERSEAS OR SOMETHING?

YEP, UP THERE IN HEAVEN.
ACTUALLY, IT'S *KINDA* EMBARRASSIN' TO ADMIT, BUT I HAD SOME PRETTY BAD GRADES FOR AN ANGEL.
HOPEFULLY STUDYIN' ABROAD'LL HELP ME ON MY NEXT TEST.
UH-HUH... *RIGHT*.

OKAY, THAT'S IT! I CAN'T TAKE THIS ANYMORE, MISHA-SAN!
YOU'VE GOT TO STOP SAYING THESE CRAZY THINGS! IT'S BAD ENOUGH YOU'RE STALKING ME!!
AUU-HH?
ARE YOU EVEN LISTENING TO ME?!
WHELPERS, BETTER START PREPARIN' FOR THE CELEBRATIONS!
MISHA-SAN!!
MISHA-SA-
Shuffle
Shuffle
Slam
......
NOTE TO SELF: REMIND HER AGAIN BEFORE THE NIGHT'S OVER.
HUH? WHAT'S THIS BOX?
To: Heaven
......?
PHEW.
HEY, MISHA-SAN! I GOT THE MAJOR STUFF CLEANED UP!
WAIT... WHAT THE HECK AM I DOING?
I've got exams!
EWW! THANK YA, THANK YA! SU!!

I'M ALL SET ON MY END TOO! SU!
......!
UM...
...WHAT'S WITH THE OUTFIT?
TEE HEE HEE!
AWWW! YOU SO SILLY SILLY, KOTAROU-KUN.

REMEMBER WHAT I SAID WHEN I MET YA? YOU KNOW, THAT I'D BE YOUR NEW MOMMA?
UH, I REMEMBER REFUSING THAT OFFER.
BUT I'LL BE A GOOD ONE! YEP, EVEN DID A *TON* OF RESEARCH.
I NEVER ASKED YOU TO DO–
AWWW! DON'T BE SHY, KOTAROU-KUN!! I BET YOU'RE JUST EMBARRASSED, AREN'T YA? SU? ♡ ♡
ACTUALLY, NO. I'M NOT!
I EVEN GOTCHA A *SUPER* DELUXE SUSHI TRAY! YEP, GOTTA CELEBRATE WITH SUSHI!
DID I WOW YA WITH MY RESEARCHES OR WHAT?
ALL RIGHT, I GET IT. SO YOU STUDIED. WAY TO GO.
OHHH, BUT THERE'S ONE LAST THING THAT A CELEBRATION CAN'T DO WITHOUT...

TA-DA!!
清酒
*Chrysanthemum Sake
OH, YOU HOLD ONE TOO, 'KAY?!
OKIE DOKIE, HERE WE GO!
HERE, YOU DO THE HONORS.
THIS'LL BE GREAT!
......

YAHOO!! MISHA'S GOT A NEW HOME!!
YAY! CONGRATS FOR MISHA!!
I'M AFRAID TO EVEN ASK WHERE SHE LEARNED THIS.
清酒
AWRIGHTY!
SOOO...
...SHALL WE BEGIN, KOTAROU-KUN?
HERE YOU GO.
YOU'RE KIDDING. YOU *ACTUALLY* EXPECT ME TO DRINK THAT? THAT'S *SAKE!!*
BUT ALL THE BOOKS SAID SHARING A DRINK WAS CUSTOMARY! ♪
NOW CHUG THIS SUCKER DOWN!
B-BUT I'M NOT OLD ENOUGH!
AHHH, I WON'T TELL! SU!
HEY, MOMS DON'T LET THEIR KIDS–
GACK!!

URRG-GHHH...
I'M...I'M GWONNA BE SIKK.
TEE HEE HEE HEE! UH HYO HYO HYO! NYA NYA NYAAA!
UNGH, DIS IS BAD...SO MAWCH FWAR STUDERLING TOWIGHT.
MEOW! MEOW! SQUEEK, SQUEEK.
HEY!!
MROOWR! HEE HEE!
DON'T YA KNOW I'VE GWAT EXAMS ON SAWNDAY?! DID YA EVEN HEAR MEH EAWIER?!
DWARNIT, MISHA-SHAN...S-SEWIOSILY!
MEOW?

WHY'S IT HAFTA...
...HAFTA BE ME THAT YOU–
?
URRGGHHH... I'M GWONNA BE SIKK!!
TEE HEE! YOU'RE TALKIN' FUNNY, KOTAROU-KUUUN!
IFFEN YA'S FEELIN' SICKIE WICKIE, DEN IT'S BEST TA TAKE A BREATHER.
UHGH... HUH?

YAHOO!!
WHOO, LOOKIE!! I'M ON TOP OF THE WORLD! SU!
URRGHH ...

WHA? WHY'M I OWSIDE?
....
....
ふ、
UGH... OH WELL.
....
....
WHOA, NOW THAT'S WHAT I CALL A VIEW.
YEP YEP! SU!
...!
....
WOW... PERCHED UP HERE...
...ALL THOSE IMPORTANT THINGS DON'T SEEM TO MATTER.
HUH?
LIKE EXAMS.
....
AND IT'S LIKE...
...I DON'T KNOW...

WHY AM
I DOING THIS?
WHY AM I
TRYING SO
HARD?
Sigh...

THERE, THERE.
IT'S AWRIGHT.
....
IT'LL BE AWRIGHT.
Aaahh
AACHOO!
GETTIN' A BIT CHILLY. SU.
WHY DON'T WE HEAD BACK?
HUH?

YAAHOOOOOO!!

AAH!
WAARRGGHH!!
Blink
HUH?!
Blink

......
......
I'M...I'M IN MY ROOM.
WAS IT ALL A DREAM?
MY HEAD'S... POUNDING.
HMM?
ふわ
......
......?
KOTAROU-CHAAAN!!
......

MORNIN', KOTAROU-CHAN!
HIYA!
AND, UH...GOOD MORNING, MISHA-SAN.
OH...HEY, KOBOSHI-CHAN.
HMM? YOU DON'T LOOK SO GOOD, KOTAROU-CHAN.
DID YOU NOT GET ENOUGH SLEEP LAST NIGHT?
TEE HEE HEE! KOTAROU-KUN WAS UP THE WHOLE NIGHT WITH ME! SU!!
W-W-WHAT?!
KOTAROU-CHAN!! DID THAT CRAZY WOMAN DO SOMETHING, YOU KNOW, W-WEIRD TO YOU?
UM, WELL... PROBABLY, BUT TO BE HONEST...
...I CAN'T REALLY REMEMBER WHAT ALL HAPPENED LAST NIGHT.
EWWWW!! THAT'S JUST WRONG!!

Lesson 4
How to Enjoy Halloween

TOOO... DAAY...
ISSS... ♪
...THE *LONG* AWAITED AND *MUCH* ANTICIPATED COURAGE COMPETITION!!
WHAT'S THAT YOU SAY?
WHY AM I DRESSED LIKE THIS?
EH HEH HEH! ♡
WELL, THAT'S A VERY GOOD QUESTION!
YOU SEE, THE COURAGE COMPETITION IS A SIXTH GRADE RITE OF PASSAGE.
IT DATES BACK FOREVER AND IS A DIRECT OFFSHOOT OF HALLOWEEN.
IN OTHER WORDS, IT'S AN ANYTHING GOES EX-TRAVAGANZA OF EVIL!!
AND I FOR ONE HAVE BEEN ANXIOUSLY AWAITING THIS MOMENT EVER SINCE I WAS A WEE LITTLE FIRST GRADER! ♡

JUST YOU WAIT! I'M GONNA BLAZE THROUGH AND NAB THE FASTEST TIME EVER, BABY!
OH, *REALLY?* YOU ACTUALLY EXPECT TO MAKE IT PAST ALL THE TRAPS SET BY YOURS TRULY?!
....
EH? WHAT'S UP WITH HIM?
....
OH, H-HE'S NOT TOO KEEN ON THE WHOLE GORE FEST.
RIGHT?
Y-YEAH—
HOWDY! WHEE!

HEY THERE, CUTIE.
LIL' 'OL ME? A CUTIE? ♪
TEE HEE HEE HEE, KOTAROU-KUN'S SOOO CUUTE!!
ARGH!!
OH, KOTAROU-CHAN. EVERY-THING'LL BE OKAY. PROMISE.
....
WHAT'S DA MATTER? SU?
MATTER? AH, IT'S JUST WE'RE DOING OUR COURAGE COMPETITION OVER AT THE TEMPLE TONIGHT AND—
Oh, shoot.
WHOOPS, IXNAY ON THE INFOYAY! 'KAY, UM, LOOK, MISHA-SAN...
THIS IS ONLY FOR SIXTH GRAD-ERS! NO MIDDLE SCHOOLERS ALLOWED!! GOT IT?!
LIKE THAT'LL STOP HER.

THE TEMPLE ...
...AT NIGHT, HUH?
I JUST...
...I JUST DON'T LIKE IT.
I HATE BEING SCARED. I HATE IT!
AND SO THAT NIGHT...
LISTEN UP! EACH PERSON'LL START RIGHT HERE ALONE AND WORK THEIR WAY UP TO THE TEMPLE.
Goal
Forest
Embankment
Start
ALL ALONG THE WAY YOU'LL ENCOUNTER VARIOUS *ATTRACTIONS* THAT WE, THE ACTION COMMITTEE, HAVE DEVISED.
ALSO, THERE'S A SLOPE TO THE LEFT. SO STAY ON THE PATH!
THE FASTEST TIMES GET PRIZES AND CERTIFICATES... IF YOU SURVIVE!

OH MAN! THIS IS GONNA BE SO AWESOME!!
HEH HEH HEH! JUST WAIT'LL YOU SEE WHAT I HAVE IN STORE FOR YOU, TEN-CHAN!
HERE, KOTAROU-CHAN. ALL YOU GOTTA DO IS WEAR THIS, GOT IT?
ERR, UM, YEAH.
SO SHE FINALLY ROPED YOU INTO THE ACTION COMMITTEE, EH?
HOPE THE SCARE TACTICS DON'T GET TOO MUCH FOR YA, MAN.
I'M STILL NOT TOO KEEN ON THIS WHOLE CONCEPT.
WELL, TRUST ME, YOU WON'T LIVE IT DOWN IF ANY OF THE GIRLS SEE YOU WETTING YOUR PANTS!
Ha Ha Ha
Ha Ha Ha
TRUST ME. I *NEVER* WET MY PANTS.
PSSSSSSSSSSS
ARGH, GROSS! G-GET AWAY FROM ME MAN!
Please, don't leave me alone!!
OKIES, EVERYONE! PLACES!! IT'S SHOW-TIME!!
HOW EMBARRASSING.
WHY AM I SUCH A SCAREDY-CAT?
ON YOUR MARK!
GET SET... GO!

UUGGAAHH!!
HMPH. IS THAT THE BEST YOU'VE GOT?
SCOOORRRE !!
HIIYARRGH!!

BWA HA HA! THAT'S WHAT YOU GET FOR NOT TAKING THIS SERIOUSLY, *SUCKAH!!*
......
NOW, WHO SHALL BE OUR NEXT *VICTIM?*
WAH!
W-WHAT'S THE MATTER, KOTAROU-CHAN?
UH, IT'S N-NOTHING. S-SORRY.
WELL, IF YOU SAY SO.
UGH... EVEN THE SHADOWS ARE FREAKING ME OUT.
WHA?!
Rustle
WHAT ON EARTH?!
IS SOME-ONE OUT THERE?!

TEE HEE HEE HEE!
♡
WHA-M-MISHA-SAN?! YOU'RE HERE?!
AND WHAT'S WITH THE CRAZY GET-UP?!

HMM? YOU MEAN DIS THING? SU?
WELL, I FIGURED I'D STOP BY AND HELP CHEER ON KOTAROU-KUUUN.
WAIT A MINUTE, SISTER, I THOUGHT I TOLD YO—
......
KOTA, KOTA, KOTAROU-KUN! GO, KOTAROU-KUUUN!
WHAT THE?
ARRRGHHH!! CUT IT OUT!!
AWRIGHT, AWRIGHT! WE GET IT!! NOW GET OVER HERE AND ZIP IT, WILL YA?!
NO PUSHY-WUSHY, MEANIE!
Phew!
Okie dokie smokie! Rrroger dat, cap'n! And go, go, Kotarou-kun!
Hush! Stop talking!!
SHEESH!
THAT MISHA GIRL'S GOT ISSUES.

JEEZ, I SHOULDA KNOWN SHE'D SHOW UP.
YARGH!!
ALL RIGHT!! ANOTHER ONE BITES THE DUST!!
LESSEE, VICTIM NUMBER 27...DEAD.
Fret
Fret
....
....
SAY, WHY ARE YOU SO SCARED BY THIS STUFF, ANYWAY?
HUH? UM...
WELL, IT'S... YOU KNOW...
OH WELL, I GUESS NOBODY'S PERFECT.
SOMEONE'S COMIN'!
FOR REAL?
....
I JUST WANTED TO CRAWL IN A HOLE AND HIDE.
!

......
WHA? A GIRL?
UGGH...
...MY HEAD'S POUNDING!
KOBOSHI, IS SHE ONE OF YOUR "ATTRACTIONS"?

!?
UWAAAHHHHH!!
......
!
TEE HEE HEE HEE.

KOTAROU-CHAN?
I'M *BACK!* AND ALL CHANGED! SU!
?
WHERE'D KOTAROU-CHAN GO?

HUH?
THE EMBANKMENT?
LET'S SEE, FIRST THERE WAS THIS GIRL...
...AND THEN THAT GUST OF WIND AND THEN I WAS HERE. WEIRD.
OH NO, THE COURAGE COMPETITION!
URRRM...
I *REALLY* DON'T WANNA CLIMB THROUGH ALL THAT.
BUT I NEED TO GET BACK TO KOBOSHI-CHAN.
....
PHEW, MADE IT UP.

!!
WAAHHHH!!
AAAAHHHHH!!
UWAAGGHH!!
HEEELP!

......
KOBOSHI-CHAN, W-WHY?
I made those!
JEEZ, I DON'T KNOW WHAT'S WORSE... KOBOSHI-CHAN'S TRAPS...
...OR THE REAL DEAL.
AT ANY RATE, I HAVE TO FIND SOME-ONE...
...AND FIND THEM QUICK!
PLEASE, I DON'T WANT TO BE ALONE...
I HATE BEING ALONE.
UWWAAHHHHH!!

AH, THERE YOU ARE! TEE HEE!
......
UM, KO...
...KOTAROU-KUN?!
....
OH, M-MISHA-SAN...
......
I'M REALLY...
...REALLY SORRY THAT I...
...I CAN'T HANDLE THIS STUFF VERY WELL.

ARE YOU FEELING A LITTLE BETTER NOW?
YEAH, A LITTLE.
......
UGH, SORRY FOR THE TROUBLE.
HMM?
IT'S SAD, ISN'T IT?
......

REMEMBER I TOLD YOU MY MOM PASSED AWAY?
UM, IT WAS A CAR ACCIDENT.
I WAS WITH HER AT THE TIME...
I...I SURVIVED, BUT SHE...
...SHE DIED ON IMPACT.
IT'S AN IMAGE YOU NEVER FORGET.
MOM JUST LYING THERE...
......
...AND THE COLOR OF HER BLOOD.
......
......
......
I SHOULD TELL YOU...
I... SEE THESE THINGS.
YOU KNOW, STUFF THAT NO ONE ELSE CAN.
MY MOM USED TO ALWAYS BE THERE TO COMFORT ME AND TELL ME NOT TO BE AFRAID.
AFTER SHE DIED, I...I JUST GOT WORSE AND...
....
HEH. PATHETIC, AIN'T IT?

きゅ
Squeeze
WELL, I SUPPOSE IF YOU'RE WITH ME...
...THEN YOU WON'T EVER HAVE TO BE SCARED AGAIN. SU.
....
MI...
...MISHA-SAN?!

!
AH!
WHA?!
M-MISHA-SAN?!
MISHA-SAN, WHAT'S WRONG?!
AAAHH! IT'S MY HEAD...IT HURTS!
MISHA-SA-

......!
AGGHH !!
!!
EEEK!
YEEEK!
....
......

STAY AWAY!!
......
I...I'M SORRY.

DO
HEY, MISHA-SAN?
ARE YOU ALL RIGHT?
NYA?
......
PHEW!
......
HAAAHHH!! I'M SOOO SOOO SORRY! SU!! I DON'T KNOW WHAT CAME OVER ME! SU!!
WHA?! SPEAK TO ME, KOTAROU-KUN! SPEAK TO ME! SU!!
I-I'M FINE!
REALLY !!
OH, THANK GOODNESS!
THANK GOODIE GOODIE GOODNESS! SU!!
SO, UM...
...DON'T WORRY... OKAY?
... DON'T ...

AH! FINALLY, WE MADE IT.
EWW!! THERE THEY ARE! SEE 'EM?!
KOBOSHI-CHAN, IT'S OVER?
GOOD, YOU MADE IT! WHERE'D YOU GET OFF TOO?
YO, GUYS! WHAT'S UP?
SO, DIDJA HEAR? I CAME IN FIRST, BABY!
WHOA, NICE ONE, TEN-CHAN.
BOO! I DEMAND A RECOUNT!!
AND TONIGHT'S WINNER! CLASS 6-4'S TAKASHI AYANOKOJI!!.
WOO HOO!! YEAH!!
AND FOR HIS EFFORTS HE'LL RECEIVE...
...A SET OF FOUR FREE PASSES TO THE HELLISH INN!!
1
2
3
4
AWRIGHTY!! NEXT SUNDAY WE'RE ALL MEETIN' UP AND WE'RE GONNA SHOW THOSE GHOSTS A THING OR TWO!!
YAY YAY!!
WHA?!
N-NO WAY!!
BOO!!

How to Pleasantly Spend a Rainy Day

EIGHTH?!
BUT AREN'T THESE THE MOCK TEST RESULTS?
HOLY COW, TEN-CHAN! YOU'RE EIGHTH IN THE NATION?!
SHEESH, UEMATSU! YOU NEED A MUZZLE OR SOMETHIN'?!
BUT YOU DON'T EVEN GO TO REVIEW! HOW'D YOU DO THAT?!
ALL YOU EVER DO IN CLASS IS SLEEP!
SO I GOT LUCKY. WHAT'S THE BIG DEAL?!
YOU CAN GO ANYWHERE YOU WANT WITH SCORES LIKE THAT!
WAIT, THAT MEANS YOU GOT A-RANKINGS IN EVERY SUBJECT! I GOTTA SEE THIS!
JEEZ, CAN YOU GET ANY MORE ANNOYING?!
JUST SHOW ME AWREADY !!

I GUESS TEN-CHAN JUST STUDIES REALLY HARD AT HOME.
Kotarou is jealous.
......
I'LL SEE YOU GUYS LATER.
HEY, WAIT UP! WE'RE COMING!
TEE HEE HEE HEE HEE!!
GYAAHHH!!
......
WHAT ARE YOU? A NINJA?! WHERE DO YOU KEEP APPEARING FROM?!
TEE HEE HEE! YA SEEN KOTAROU-KUN AROUND? SU?
SORRY, BUT YOU JUST MISSED 'IM!
TEE HEE HEE!
TEE HEE HEE.
WOULD YOU KINDLY UNHAND KOTAROU-CHAN THIS INSTANT?!
SEE YA, TEN-CHAN.
CIAO, BABE.

AH...
HEY!
HOW'S IT GOIN'?

SHE A FRIEND OF YOURS, TEN-CHAN?
YEAH, KINDA.
WE ACTUALLY JUST MET THIS MORNING.
I HAD LOST A CONTACT AT THE TRAIN STATION...
...AND THIS LOVELY LADY WAS KIND ENOUGH TO HELP ME FIND IT.
IT'S THAT GIRL AGAIN! GRRR!
I CAN'T THANK YOU ENOUGH FOR HELPING ME, MISS.
SO, YOU BUSY THIS AFTERNOON?
POUND
THROB

SO...WE MEET AGAIN.
STAY AWAY!
......
G-GUESS SO.
OOH LA LA! YOU GUYS KNEW EACH OTHER, HUH?
NO, IT'S NOT–
KOTAROU, YOU STUD! FIRST MISHA AND NOW HER?! WHOA!

MY NAME IS...
...SHIA.
....
K-KOTAROU...
...HIGUCHI.
HOW VERY NICE TO MEET YOU...
...HIGUCHI-SAN.
ACK! MY HEAD!
....
IF YOU DON'T MIND ME ASKING...
...WHEN MIGHT YOUR BIRTHDAY BE, HIGUCHI-SAN?
........?
MARCH.
IT'S MARCH 26TH.

ぽん
HERE. IT'S A PRIMROSE.
!

IT MEANS, "FIRST LOVE."
AND IT'S THE BIRTH FLOWER FOR THOSE WITH YOUR BIRTHDAY.
WHOA, SWEET! YOU A MAGICIAN OR SOMETHIN'?
HELLO THERE, I'M KOBOSHI UEMATSU.
ARE YOU NEW HERE?
HEY, HEY, SHIA-SAN!
DO THAT TRICK AGAIN! DO IT AGAIN!
OH, NO! MISHA-SAN!
WHAT'S WRONG WITH HER?
!
WE GOTTA SPLIT!

UM, WE'RE NOT FEELING WELL. SO, WE'LL BE AT THE NURSE'S OFFICE!
BYE!
DO YOU THINK THAT I...
...I MIGHT HAVE UPSET HIM?
NAH, DON'T YOU WORRY ABOUT HIM!
HE'S ALWAYS BEEN A RUDE LITTLE SNOT.

*Nurse's Office
保健
OH...
I SEE.
HELLO? ANYBODY HERE?
LOOKS LIKE THE NURSE STEPPED OUT.
WHY IS IT THAT...
...AROUND THAT GIRL...
......

KOTAROU-KUN! WHEE!
WHHAA?!
KOTAROU-KUN!!
GIVE IT UP, MISHA-SAN!
JUST LIE DOWN ALREADY!
UNY-AAA?
......
YOU FEEL IT TOO.
DON'T YOU, MISHA-SAN?
HUH?

THERE'S SOMETHING ABOUT HER.
ポツ
HMM, I'M NOT THAT SURE WHAT YA'S TALKIN' ABOUT! SU!
ARE YOU SERIOUS?!
......
EWW, PWETTY FLOWER!
THAT THING? SHIA-SAN GAVE IT TO ME. YOU WERE ZOMBIFIED, WEREN'T YOU?
TEE HEE HEE HEE! IT'S SO PRETTY! SU!
YOU CAN HAVE IT IF YOU WANT.
AWW, I COULDN'T. BUT WE CAN SHARE IT! SHARING IS CARING!
......

ゴロゴロ
!
......!!
A BLACK-OUT?!
OR MAYBE NOT.
THAT'S STRANGE.
IT WAS SUNNY A FEW MINUTES AGO.
UGGH!

......!
THIS HEADACHE... IT HAS TO BE...
SHE'S NOT THERE.
BUT I FEEL HER. SHIA-SAN'S CLOSE BY.
......
I NEED TO CHECK.
ARE YOU...
...LEAVING ME? SUUUUU?
SEE IF THEY'RE STILL OUTSIDE.
KOTAROU-KUN?

NAAHHH.
ふ
ぽ
WHY'D THEY BE OUTSIDE STILL?
'SIDES, IT'S RAINING.
THAT AND, WELL...
...I THOUGHT YOU WEREN'T FEELING WELL.
ちら
ふい

DON'T YA HAVE REVIEW TONIGHT?!
REVIEW? UH, NOT TONIGHT.
SOUNDS LIKE THE RAIN'S...
...REALLY COMING DOWN, HUH?
"MOCK EXAM"?
MOCK ENTRANCE EXAMINA-TION.
PHEW! I'M SO GLAD! YIPPIE!
DON'T BE. I TOTALLY BOMBED MY MOCK EXAM.
......
......
......
HMM? EIGHTH? SU?
NOTHING.
EIGHTH, MAN. JEEZ.
......
HE BARELY STUDIES.

OKIES, HOW'S ABOUT WE JUST LAY HERE...
...LIKE THIS UNTIL THE RAIN STOPS? PITTER PATTER.
HUH?

TEE HEE HEE HEE. WANNA PLAY STEAM-ROLLER?
!
OH, KOTAROU-KUUUN.
......
WHERE YA GOIN'?
MAYBE I...I SHOULD LOOK OVER MY TEST BOOKLET.
FIGURE OUT MY MISTAKES BEFORE THE NEXT ONE.
OH? THERE'S ANOTHER ONE? SU?
OKIES, THEN HOW'S ABOUT I HELP YOU TO STUDY INSTEAD? SU?
AND HOW ARE YOU GONNA DO THAT?
I'LL FIND A WAY!
......
LOOKIT THE RAIN!
IT'S LIKE A WATER-FALL OUT THERE, HUH?
すちゃっ
MIGHT HAVE TO FINALLY BUY AN UMBRELLA.

YAAHOO!!
TEE HEE HEE HEE!
WHA?!
MISHA-SAN!
WHAT ARE YOU, NUTS?! IT'S POURING!

I ONCE READ THAT IF YOU GO UNDER A WATER-FALL AND WISH REAL HARD...
...YOU'RE WISH'LL COME TRUE! SU!
......
さあっ
WELL, I WISH THAT YOU GET...
...A *REALLY* GREAT SCORE ON YOUR NEXT TESTIE-WESTIE! WHEE!

は
COME ON, YOU'RE GOING TO GET SICK OUT HERE.
AWW, YOU LIKE ME! YOU REALLY LIKE ME!
LISTEN...
...I'LL MAKE SURE YOUR WISH COMES TRUE.
BUT I'LL DO IT BY MYSELF...BY TRYING HARDER.

OKIE DOKIE! YAY!
HERE! SU.
......
さ、

MORNIN', KOTAROU-CHAAAN!!

OH MY GOSH! KOTAROU-CHAN, YOU'RE SICK?!
UM, YEAH...I GUESS SO.
AND IT'S ALL MY FAULT! I'M SO SOWWY!!
GET YOUR PAWS OFFA HIM!!
I-IT'S OKAY.
IS THERE ANYTHING I CAN DO TO EASE YOUR SUFFERING? SU?
REALLY, I'LL BE FINE.
YOU SHOULD BE HOME IN BED.
Y'KNOW, THEY SAY YOU CAN LOSE YOUR COLD BY GIVING IT TO SOMEONE ELSE.
OH HEY, YOU TWO! WHAT'S UP?
HEY, I CAN HELP! GIVE YER COLDIE WOLDIE TO ME!
TEE HEE HEE HEE HEE! JUST TELL ME HOW I STARTS THE COLD TRANSFERRIN' STUFF! WEE HEE!
MISHA-SAN! GET BACK!! BACK, I SAY!!

Lesson 6

How to Enjoy Oneself at the Hot Springs: Part 1

ポ
ト
AWWW, TEN-CHAN. LOST AGAIN, EH?
QUIET, YOU.
WELL, IT'S THE TRUTH, KLEENEX MAN!
HEY, A PRIZE IS A PRIZE.
AND WHAT ABOUT THE RICE CRACKERS I WON EARLIER?!
WAIT, I'VE GOT SOME RAFFLE TICKETS TOO.
OOH, NICE ONE, KOTAROU.
COME ON. WIN US THAT HOT SPRINGS VACATION, MAN!
......
泉旅行
(ペア)
セット
ガラ ガラ
AND SEVENTH PRIZE, A POCKET PACK OF TISSUES.
......
AWW, SHUCKS.

KOTAROU-KUUUUN!
WHA-WHAT WERE YOU THINKING, MISHA-SAN?! ARE YOU TRYING TO KILL HIM?!
KOTAROU-CHAN, SPEAK TO ME!!
TEE HEE HEE.
PLEASE, GET OFF OF ME.
I'VE TOLD YOU A HUNDRED TIMES TO STOP GLOMPING ON TO KOTAROU-CHAN!!
UNYA?
ARE YOU EVEN HEARING WHAT I'M SAYING?!
AND YOU! WHY CAN'T YOU JUST TELL HER OFF?!
BUT I HAVE.
TEE HEE HEE HEE. SO, WHAT'S YA UP TA? SU?
THIS? IT'S A PRIZE DRAWING.
WHOA!
I WANNA DO IT TOO!
UH, IF YOU WANT TO. HERE, BE MY GUEST.
HOPE YA GET A KLEENEX.
YAY!

コロ
Plop
Plop
コロ
AH!
B-BUT THAT'S IMPOSSIBLE!!
HOLY COW!! TWO FIRST PRIZES?!
THAT'S FOUR HOT SPRINGS VACATION TICKETS!
OKIES, HOW'S ABOUT WE ALLA GO! SU?!
WHA?!
すたっ
わいわい
たたたっ

ニャー
ニャー
ニャー
YAHOO! HERE WE ARE! SU!!
DA HOT SPRINGSA! SU!!

THANKS, SIR!! WE'LL TAKE IT FROM HERE!
THAT'S IT. WE'RE ALL CHECKED IN.
WHICH ROOMS DID WE GET?
LESSEE, THE MAPLE ROOM ON THE THIRD FLOOR AND THE WISTERIA ON THE FIRST.
WHICH ONE DO YOU WANT?
I WANNA SLEEPY WITH KOTAROU-KUN! WHOOPIE!
RAWWWWR!!
EVEN IF THIS PLACE'S CRAZY ENOUGH TO ALLOW THAT, I SURE AS HECK WON'T!!
WELL, UM, OKAY.
LOOKIE HERE, YOU'RE ROOMIN' WITH ME! CAPICHE?!
OH, OKIE-DOKIE.
RRROGER THAT! SU!!
AH, WE ALL KNOW HOW MUCH YOU LIKE MISHA-SAN.
JUST KEEP IT UP, TEN-CHAN, AND I'LL POP Y–

OH, HOW PERFECT! I REALLY, REALLY LIKE YOU TOO! SU!!
OKIES THEN, SHALL WE?
ARGH! MY NECK!! OWW! OWW! LEMME GO!! HELP
NEVER A DULL MOMENT, HUH?
LET'S JUST FIND OUR ROOM.

WOO HOO!!
I WANT THIS SIDE! WHEE!
WHOA, CHECK IT OUT!! THE VIEW'S AMAZIN'! TEE HEE!!
JEEZ, CAN'T SHE EVER SIT STILL?!
UGH, THIS IS GOING TO BE A LONG TRIP.
THEN AGAIN, ROOMING WITH KOTAROU-CHAN WOULDN'T BE GOOD EITHER.
IT'S LIKE SHE'S NEVER BEEN IN A HOTEL BEFORE.
SHE ACTS LIKE, I DUNNO...
...SUCH A CHILD.
KOBOSHI-CHAN?
I MADE SOME TEA.
OH.
UH, THANKS.
I HOPE YOU DON'T MIND...
...BUT CAN I CALL YOU "KOBOSHI-CHAN"?
EH?

ぷは——っ
I GIVE UP.
KOBOSHI-CHAN!
YES, WHAT IS IT?
WELL, WE DON'T GET TO TALK THAT MUCH, SO...
...I WAS HOPING WE COULD CHAT A LITTLE WHILE. SU.
SO, WHAT KINDA STUFF DO YOU LIKE TO DO, KOBOSHI-CHAN?
UH, I...I LIKE VIDEO GAMES.
AND I'M TAKING BALLET AND LEARNING PIANO AND VIOLIN RIGHT NOW.
WHOA, REALLY? THAT'S SO COOLIE-COOL!
OH, IT'S NOTHING SPECIAL. REALLY.
STILL, YOU'RE A BUSY, BUSY GIRLIE-GIRL!
WHAT ABOUT YOU? WHAT DO YOU LIKE?
HUH?

THE WIND.
HUH?
WHEN I STAND AGAINST THE WIND...
...IT SWEEPS OVER ME AND IT MAKES ME WANNA FLY. HEE HEE.
......
BIZAR-RO.
SO, OUT OF ALL THE STUFF YOU LIKE TO DO...
...IS THERE ONE THING YOU WANNA GROW UP AND DO? SU?

HUH? UM...I DUNNO.
I NEVER REALLY THOUGHT ABOUT IT.
UH, WHAT ABOUT YOU, MISHA-SAN?
TEE HEE HEE.
I HOPE TO BECOME A FULL-FLEDGED ANGEL ONE DAY.
AN "ANGEL"?
WHAT KIND OF OCCUPATION IS THAT?
AND...
WHEN I DO BECOME ONE...
...I WANNA WORK MY HARDEST...
TO MAKE YOU AND EVERYONE ELSE HAPPY! WHEE!
......
YOU WANT TO MAKE OTHER PEOPLE HAPPY...
...AND NOT YOURSELF?
OH, NO. IF I'M NOT HAPPY...
...THEN I WOULDN'T BE ABLE TO MAKE ANYONE ELSE HAPPY EITHER. SU.

AND THAT WOULD BE MY DREAM JOB. TEE HEE.
....
UGH, IT'S LOOKIN' PRETTY BAD OUT THERE.
WHA? NO WAY! YOU'RE STUDYING?!
WELL, I DID SKIP REVIEW TODAY.
WHO THE HECK STUDIES WHEN THEY'RE ON VACATION, MAN?!
WE'RE NOT ALL NATURAL BRAINS LIKE YOU.
......

HIYA! SURPRISEY-WISEY!
UWAAAHH!
TEE HEE HEE HEE.
TEN-CHAN? KOTAROU-CHAN?
WAIT A SEC! WHAT ARE YOU DOIN' UNDER THERE, MISHA-SAN?!
TEE HEE HEE HEE.

LET'S GO...
...TAKE A BATHIE-WATHIE!
HEY, GOOD IDEA. LET'S GO HIT THE HOT SPRINGS BEFORE IT STARTS RAINING!
TEE HEE HEE.
YOU CAN'T ARGUE WITH THAT, CAN YA?
AH, WHY NOT?
SPEAKING OF BATHS...
...THE GUY AT THE LOBBY WAS TELLIN' ME THAT...

...THE OUTDOOR SPRINGS HERE ARE CO-ED.
WHAAAAAAT?!
TRUST ME, YOU COULDN'T PAY ME ENOUGH TO BATHE WITH YOU.
WHAT WAS THAT?! GET BACK HERE, TEN-CHAN!! YOU'RE A DEAD MAN!!
OKAY, OKAY! I TAKE IT BACK! SHEESH!!

かぽーーーん
WOWW-WEE!!
LOOKS LIKE NOBODY'S HERE YET.
ホ
HMM... GOOD.
KOBOSHI-CHAN, YOU WANT ME TO WASH YOUR BACK? SU?
UH, YOU DON'T MIND?
ざーーー
OH PLEASE, OH PLEASE, DON'T LET THEM WALK IN!
ちゃぽーーーん
IT'S NO USE.
I JUST CAN'T RELAX.
IT MUST BE NICE NOT TO HAVE A BRAIN.

AHHHH!
......
......
MAN, SHE'S SO PRETTY.

THE WATER'S JUST RIGHT, HUH? ♪
WHA?
UM, Y-YES. UH, IT IS.
......
......
COME ON, MAN! THEY'VE GOTTA BE DONE BY NOW! I'M GOIN' IN!!
TEN-CHAN?!
BUT WE JUST GOT IN!!
I CAN'T LET THOSE GUYS SEE ME NAKED!!
I HAVE TO...HAVE TO GET OUT...OF–

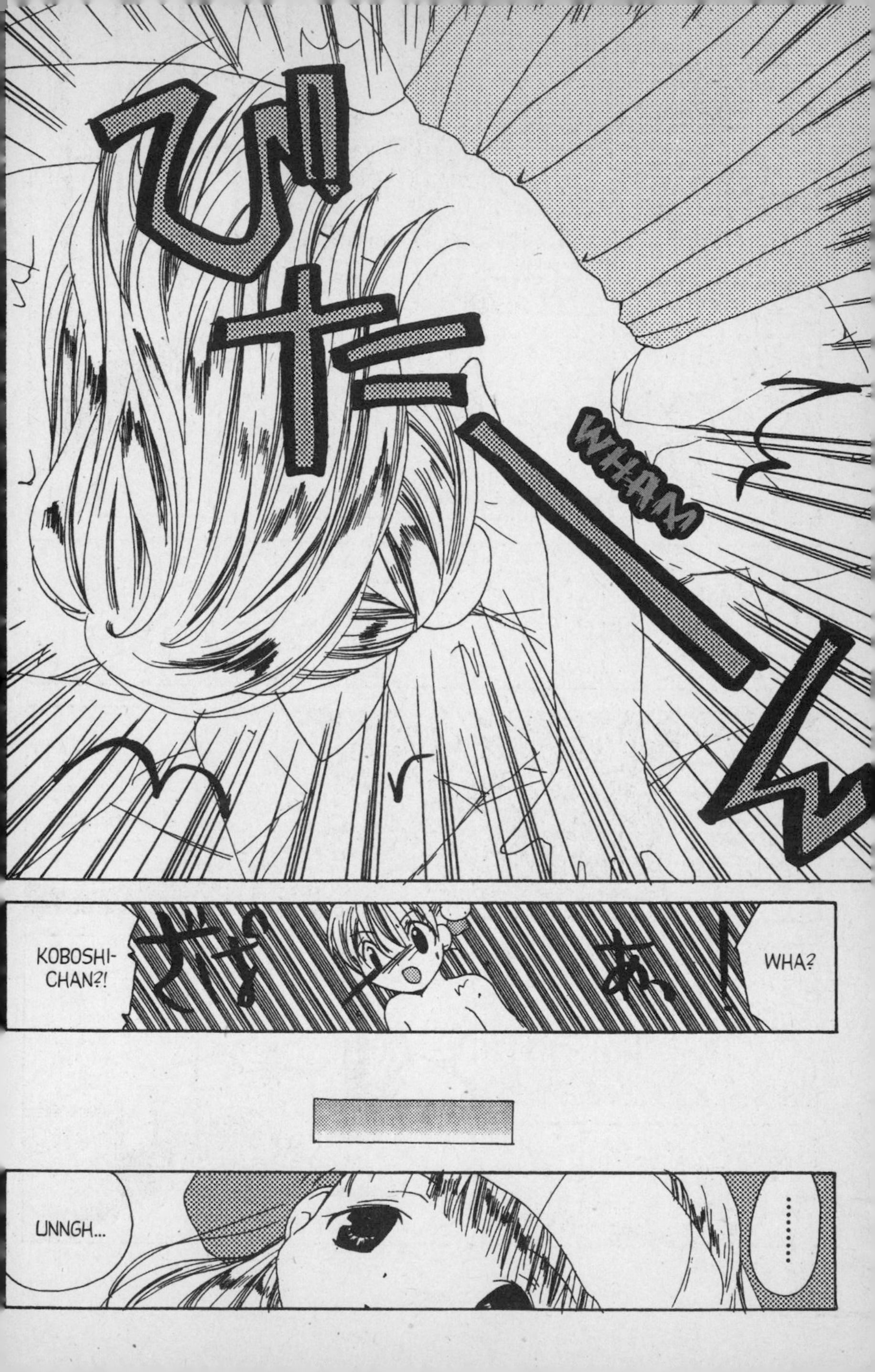

びたーん
WHAM
WHA?
KOBOSHI-CHAN?!
......
UNNGH...

AH, GOOD.
YOU'RE AWAKE.
W-WHERE AM I?
IN OUR HOTEL ROOM.
YOU HIT YOUR HEAD AND WE HAD TO CARRY YOU OUT.
DOH!
UGH, I SEE.
THERE GOES THE WEEK-END.
I SENT MISHA-SAN TO GET YOU SOME ICE.
AND TEN-CHAN WENT TO THE FRONT FOR SUPPLIES.
NOT SURE WHAT MISHA-SAN WAS THINKING. SHE RAN OUT TOTALLY NAKED.
WHAT?!
S-SO, YOU SAW HER, THEN?
UM, UH, BUT SHE DID PUT A TOWEL ON YOU.
AT LEAST I DIDN'T SEE *YOU*, RIGHT?

ぱた
ぱた
ぱた
ぱた

ぱた
ぱた
WHEN I STAND AGAINST THE WIND...
...IT SWEEPS OVER ME AND IT MAKES ME WANNA FLY. TEE HEE.
ぱた
ぱた
....
I GOTS THE ICE TEA! BRRR!
I'M SORRY ABOUT ALL THIS.
I REALLY RUINED THE WEEKEND, HUH?
....
OH, I KNOW THAT I...I TALK TOO MUCH...
...AND I'M KINDA UGLY...
AND, ARGH, I'M STUPID.
I'M SORRY FOR ALL THE TROUBLE.
I'M SO SORRY...

DON'T BE. YOU'RE NONE OF THOSE THINGS.
BESIDES, OUT OF ALL THE GIRLS I KNOW, YOU'RE THE ONE I LIKE THE MOST, KOBOSHI-CHAN.
I MEAN, YOU'RE THE ONE...
...THAT I TALK TO THE MOST.

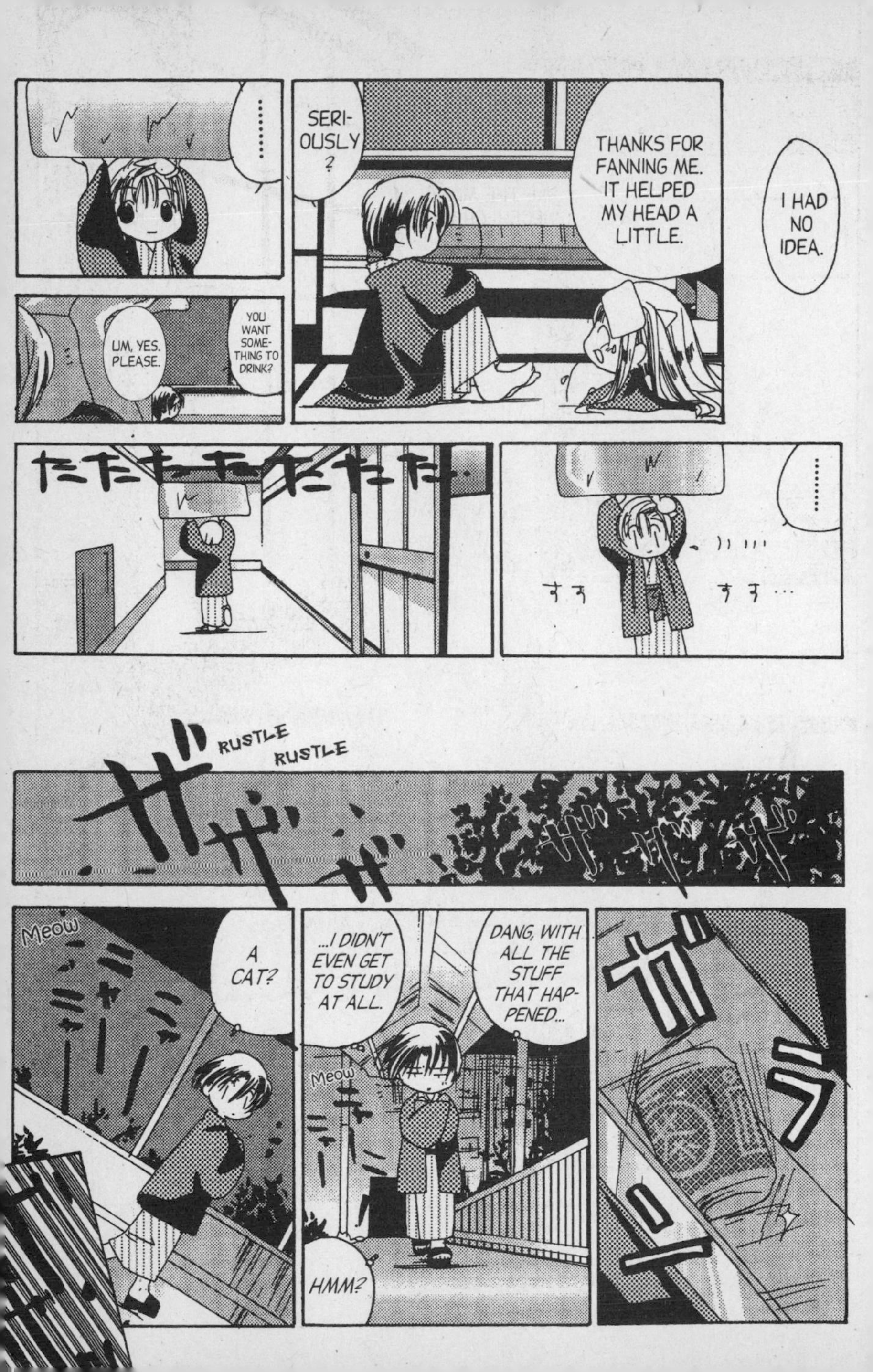
I HAD NO IDEA.
THANKS FOR FANNING ME. IT HELPED MY HEAD A LITTLE.
SERIOUSLY?
......
YOU WANT SOMETHING TO DRINK?
UM, YES. PLEASE.
......
RUSTLE RUSTLE
DANG, WITH ALL THE STUFF THAT HAPPENED...
...I DIDN'T EVEN GET TO STUDY AT ALL.
Meow
HMM?
A CAT?
Meow

Lesson 7

How to Enjoy Oneself at the Hot Springs: Part 2

WHO THE--?!
WHACK!
CAN'T... BREATHE!

......
SH...
SHIA-SAN?
......
IF YOU'RE EXPECTING AN APOLOGY... DON'T.
YOU STARTED THIS.
......
I UNDER-STAND.
ズキ…
ズキ…
......
す
KYA!
WAIT! DON'T HURT--
IT'S COLD. IT'LL HELP THE SWELL-ING.
......
I-I'M SORRY.
......
SO, SHIA-SAN...

...WHY ARE YOU HERE?

WHATCHA DOING VEGGIN' IN THE HALL, MISHA-SAN?
TEE HEE HEE HEE.
WELL, KOBOSHI-CHAN SEEMED SO HAPPY JUST NOW.
AND I JUST FELT SO HAPPY FOR HER! SU!
OH MY, OH MY, OH MY.
TEE HEE HEE HEE.
?
UH, SURE, WHATEVER. LET'S GET BACK NOW.
UM, BUT, UM, WEEEE!

YO, UEMATSU! HOW YA FEELIN'?
HEY, TEN-CHAN. MUCH BETTER.
THANKS.
SAY, WHERE'S KOTAROU?
HE WENT TO GET SOME DRINKS.
AH, COOL.
WELL, HOPE HE GET'S BACK SOON.
ME TOO.
BRING ON THE FOUR-SOME!
CAUSE WE'RE HAVIN' A MAHJONG ALL-NIGHTER, BABY!!
NO WAY! UH-UH! AIN'T GONNA HAPPEN!!
BESIDES AT A HOT SPRING... IT'S CUSTOMARY TO DO KARAOKE.
KARA-OKE?!
WHO IN THEIR RIGHT MIND WOULD THINK THAT KARAOKE IS FUN?!
I SAY WE'RE DOIN' KARAOKE! BESIDES, KOTAROU-CHAN LOVES KARAOKE TOO, SO THERE!

I-I'M HEADING BACK NOW.

YOU SEEM TO BE ENJOYING YOUR-SELVES...
...QUITE A LOT ON THIS TRIP.
......!
COME... THIS WAY, PLEASE.
YOU SEE, I-I'VE ALWAYS BEEN BY MYSELF.
....
BUT YOU KNOW, I'VE BEEN HERE BEFORE.
TO THIS VERY PLACE...A LONG, LONG TIME AGO.
....
GOSH. IT FEELS SO NICE TO BE BACK.
AARRR!
I'VE BEEN THINKING, SHIA-SAN.
EVER SINCE WE FIRST MET...
...WHENEVER I'M WITH YOU...
...I GET THESE HORRIBLY PAINFUL HEADACHES.
SHIA-SAN, ARE YOU—

......
I'M VERY SORRY FOR THE PAIN.
......!
BUT...
...I'M ALSO VERY HAPPY AT THE SAME TIME.
?
WHA?!
AND THAT-
BECAUSE IT MEANS THAT YOU, HIGUCHI-SAN...
...YOU *KNOW* ME.

SHIA-SAN?!
GAAHH!
I...
I'M ALL RIGHT...
I'M JUST SO... HAPPY.
I-I'VE BEEN... ALONE...FOR SO LONG NOW.
BUT NOW...
SHIA-SAN, TELL ME WHAT'S WRONG! SHIA-SAN?!
I'M SO HAPPY...
WHA...
...WHAT ARE YOU?

RGAAH!!
......!!
SHIA-SAN?!
COME ON, TELL ME WHAT'S WRONG!!
IT...H-HURTS...
HOLD ON, OKAY? LET ME GO GET HELP!
N-NO...
B-BUT...
...WHY NOT?!
AAUHH!!
SHIA-SAN!!
I, AHH... I-IT HURTS... SO MUCH!!
URGH!!
HI-HIGUCHI-SAN—

SHEESH, WHAT'S TAKING HIM SO LONG?

HE HAS BEEN GONE QUITE A WHILE, HASN'T HE?
GRAB A SEAT, MISHA-SAN. I'LL TEACH YOU HOW TO PLAY.
AWW, GOODIES! SU!!
YOU SET UP DEN AND I'LL GO FINDS KOTAROU-KUN!
I'S GOTTA FIND KOTAROU-KUN QUICKER! SU.
TEE HEE HEE HEE. THE SOONER I DO...
...THEN THE MORE PEOPLE'LL BE HAPPY AND THE MORE FUN WE CAN HAVE!
BECAUSE I...
...I AM AN ANGEL, AFTER ALL!
SO IT'S MY DUTY TO MAKE SURE THAT EVERYONE IS HAPPY HAPPY NO MATTER WHATSEY! SU!
TEE HEE HEE.
KOTAROU-KUUUN?
KOTAROU-KUUUN?
KOTAROU-KUUUN?

THA-
THUMP
BA-
DUMP

UH, K-KOTAROU-KUN?
......
EH...
H-HEY...
UM, KOTAROU-KUN?
......
WAKIE WAKIE!!
KOTAROU-KUN!!
AUHH!!
UH, KO-

AUUH.
......
DON'T WORRY...
...HE'S NOT DEAD.
HUH?
HE'S JUST HAD A LITTLE BIT...
...OF THE LIFE DRAINED OUT OF HIM. THAT'S ALL.
WHA?

......
I DO REGRET THIS, YOU KNOW.
WHEN IS HE GOING TO WAKE UP? SU?
W-WHEN IS HE...
I HONESTLY THOUGHT I ONLY TOOK A SMALL NIBBLE.
BUT PERHAPS I WASN'T ABLE TO CONTROL THE TRANSFER.
TRUTHFULLY, I DON'T KNOW WHEN HE'LL WAKE UP.
IF HE DOES AT ALL.
......
NO...
......
NO, KOTAROU-KUN...
......
NO...
......
I'M SORRY, BUT–
NO!!

ぱあっ
AHH!
パ
OH!

......
......
I-I'M SORRY...
BUT I-I'VE BEEN ALONE FOR SO LONG...
ALONE ALL THIS TIME... TRYING TO FIND... TO FIND...
THAT'S WHY I...
I COULDN'T BEAR TO DIE YET... I JUST COULDN'T.
SO I...
......
I'M SO SORRY.
THEN DON'T BE.
YOU CAN HAVE *MY* LIFE! SU!
I WON'T END UP LIKE KOTAROU-KUN.
TAKE AS MUCH AS LIKE! SU!
DON'T WORRY.

YOU'RE NOT ALONE ANYMORE.

......
NNUUH.
AHH, KOTAROU-CHAN!! YOU'RE AWAKE!
HUH?
WH-WHAT HAPPENED?
STRANGELY ENOUGH, MISHA-SAN FOUND YOU SPRAWLED OUTSIDE.
TEN BUCKS SAYS THIS INN'S BUILT ON A HELL MOUTH!
......
......
BUT BOY, OH BOY!! I'M SOOO HAPPIES THAT YOU'RES OKAY, KOTAROU-KUN! YAY!
フラ——————。
YOU LOOK HOR-RIBLE!
FEELIN' A BIT ANEMIC.
UH, RIGHT.
......
AWW, YOU DON'T HAVE TO LEAVE YET, SHIA-SAN!
EH?

GOOD EVENING.
OH...UH, HI.
HUH?
NO HEADACHE?
......
HOW ARE YOU FEELING, HIGUCHI-SAN?
UM, GOOD. I GUESS...
WELL THEN, ON THAT NOTE...
...I HAVE SOMETHING I NEED TO ATTEND TO.
YOU TAKE CARE, SHIA-SAN.
THANK YOU. YOU TOO.
SMALL WORLD, EH? NEVER THOUGHT WE'D END UP SEEING HER HERE!
HMM. YOU THINK SHE WON THE PRIZE ALSO?
......
COULD BE...

AWRIGHTY, LISTEN UP! UP ALL NIGHT MAHJONG MADNESS STARTS RIGHT AFTER DINNER, BABY!!
DON'T FORGET YOU AGREED TO DO KARAOKE ALSO, TEN-CHAN!!
......
MORNING, KOTAROU-KUN! WISE AND SHWINE!
ARGGH!!
UH, G-GOOD MORNING.
TEE HEE HEE.
OVER THAT ANEMIC THING, I SEE.
OH YES. THANKS FOR NOTICIN'! SU!
EXCUSE ME, MISHA-SAN?

YOU FORGOT YOUR LUNCH.
TEE HEE HEE HEE! OOPSIE, SILLY ME. THANK YA! SU!

TO BE CONTINUED IN VOLUME 2!

In the Next Volume of...

Can Kotarou's life ever get back to normal? Not likely. After all, he has a hyper-active angel and a benevolent demon living next door. Mayhem magnifies when Kotarou's best friend, Takashi, sprains his ankle right before the elementary school's new play is set to debut! And now Kotarou must take on the lead role as the Moon Princess Kaguya! What happens when Kotarou loses his voice just as the curtain is drawn? Can the show possibly go on? Find out in the second ultra-cute volume of *Pita-Ten!*

NEWS FLASHY-WASHY!
I AM INCWEDIBLY ADORABLE! YES, IT'S TRULY TRUE TRUE! BUT I CAN'T TAKE ALL THE CREDIT! IF YOU ARE A SMITTEN-KITTEN FOR MY DARLING LOOKS, YOU HAVE NONE OTHER THAN KOGE-DONBO TO THANK! SHE'S THE SUPER-DUPER TALENTED MANGA-KA WHO CREATED ME! AND IF I DO SAY SO MYSELF, I LOOK PURRRRRRFECT! SU!! NOT ONLY DID KOGE-DONBO CREATE ME AND EVERYONE ELSE IN *PITA-TEN,* BUT SHE ALSO CREATED THE COOLIE-COOL SERIES *DIGI CHARAT!* TEE HEE! AND I HEARD SHE'S ALL LOVEY-DOVEY OVER SOME BOY NAMED HARRY POTTER! SHE LIKES TO WRITE AND DRAW WACKY STORIES ABOUT THIS HARRY ALL THE TIME. SOUNDS LIKE SHE HAS A CRUSHY-WUSH ON HIM! I'M NOT SURE WHO THIS HARRY KID IS, BUT THERE'S *NO WAY* HE'S CUTER THAN LITTLE 'OL ME! WHEEE! RIGHT? RIGHT!! SU!! THANKS AGAIN, KOGE-DONBO, FOR MAKING ME SO UNBEWIEVABLY LOVEABLE!

ALSO AVAILABLE FROM

REALITY CHECK
REBIRTH
REBOUND
REMOTE June 2004
RISING STARS OF MANGA December 2003
SABER MARIONETTE J
SAILOR MOON
SAINT TAIL
SAIYUKI
SAMURAI DEEPER KYO
SAMURAI GIRL REAL BOUT HIGH SCHOOL
SCRYED
SGT. FROG March 2004
SHAOLIN SISTERS
SHIRAHIME-SYO: SNOW GODDESS TALES December 2004
SHUTTERBOX
SNOW DROP January 2004
SOKORA REFUGEES May 2004
SORCEROR HUNTERS
SUIKODEN May 2004
SUKI February 2004
THE CANDIDATE FOR GODDESS April 2004
THE DEMON ORORON April 2004
THE LEGEND OF CHUN HYANG
THE SKULL MAN
THE VISION OF ESCAFLOWNE
TOKYO MEW MEW
TREASURE CHESS March 2004
UNDER THE GLASS MOON
VAMPIRE GAME
WILD ACT
WISH
WORLD OF HARTZ
X-DAY
ZODIAC P.I.

NOVELS

KARMA CLUB APRIL 2004
SAILOR MOON

ART BOOKS

CARDCAPTOR SAKURA
MAGIC KNIGHT RAYEARTH
PEACH GIRL ART BOOK April 2004

ANIME GUIDES

COWBOY BEBOP ANIME GUIDES
GUNDAM TECHNICAL MANUALS
SAILOR MOON SCOUT GUIDES

CINE-MANGA™

CARDCAPTORS
FAIRLY ODD PARENTS MARCH 2004
FINDING NEMO
G.I. JOE SPY TROOPS
JACKIE CHAN ADVENTURES
KIM POSSIBLE
LIZZIE MCGUIRE
POWER RANGERS: NINJA STORM
SPONGEBOB SQUAREPANTS
SPY KIDS
SPY KIDS 3-D March 2004
THE ADVENTURES OF JIMMY NEUTRON: BOY GENIUS
TRANSFORMERS: ARMADA
TRANSFORMERS: ENERGON May 2004

TOKYOPOP KIDS

STRAY SHEEP

For more information visit www.TOKYOPOP.com

10103

ALSO AVAILABLE FROM

MANGA

.HACK//LEGEND OF THE TWILIGHT
@LARGE
A.I. LOVE YOU February 2004
AI YORI AOSHI January 2004
ANGELIC LAYER
BABY BIRTH
BATTLE ROYALE
BATTLE VIXENS April 2004
BIRTH May 2004
BRAIN POWERED
BRIGADOON
B'TX January 2004
CARDCAPTOR SAKURA
CARDCAPTOR SAKURA: MASTER OF THE CLOW
CARDCAPTOR SAKURA: BOXED SET COLLECTION 1
CARDCAPTOR SAKURA: BOXED SET COLLECTION 2 March 2004
CHOBITS
CHRONICLES OF THE CURSED SWORD
CLAMP SCHOOL DETECTIVES
CLOVER
COMIC PARTY June 2004
CONFIDENTIAL CONFESSIONS
CORRECTOR YUI
COWBOY BEBOP: BOXED SET THE COMPLETE COLLECTION
CRESCENT MOON May 2004
CREST OF THE STARS June 2004
CYBORG 009
DEMON DIARY
DIGIMON
DIGIMON SERIES 3 April 2004
DIGIMON ZERO TWO February 2004
DNANGEL April 2004
DOLL May 2004
DRAGON HUNTER
DRAGON KNIGHTS
DUKLYON: CLAMP SCHOOL DEFENDERS
DV June 2004
ERICA SAKURAZAWA
FAERIES' LANDING January 2004
FAKE
FLCL
FORBIDDEN DANCE
FRUITS BASKET February 2004
G GUNDAM
GATEKEEPERS
GETBACKERS February 2004
GHOST! March 2004
GIRL GOT GAME January 2004
GRAVITATION
GTO
GUNDAM WING
GUNDAM WING: BATTLEFIELD OF PACIFISTS
GUNDAM WING: ENDLESS WALTZ
GUNDAM WING: THE LAST OUTPOST
HAPPY MANIA
HARLEM BEAT
I.N.V.U.
INITIAL D
ISLAND
JING: KING OF BANDITS
JULINE
JUROR 13 March 2004
KARE KANO
KILL ME, KISS ME February 2004
KINDAICHI CASE FILES, THE
KING OF HELL
KODOCHA: SANA'S STAGE
LAMENT OF THE LAMB May 2004
LES BIJOUX February 2004
LIZZIE MCGUIRE
LOVE HINA
LUPIN III
LUPIN III SERIES 2
MAGIC KNIGHT RAYEARTH I
MAGIC KNIGHT RAYEARTH II February 2004
MAHOROMATIC: AUTOMATIC MAIDEN May 2004
MAN OF MANY FACES
MARMALADE BOY
MARS
METEOR METHUSELA June 2004
METROID June 2004
MINK April 2004
MIRACLE GIRLS
MIYUKI-CHAN IN WONDERLAND
MODEL May 2004
NELLY MUSIC MANGA April 2004
ONE April 2004
PARADISE KISS
PARASYTE
PEACH GIRL
PEACH GIRL CHANGE OF HEART
PEACH GIRL RELAUNCH BOX SET
PET SHOP OF HORRORS
PITA-TEN January 2004
PLANET LADDER February 2004
PLANETES
PRIEST
PRINCESS AI April 2004
PSYCHIC ACADEMY March 2004
RAGNAROK
RAGNAROK: BOXED SET COLLECTION 1
RAVE MASTER
RAVE MASTER: BOXED SET March 2004

10103

王ドロボウ JING
KING OF BANDITS
BY YUICHI KUMAKURA
TOKYOPOP®
100% AUTHENTIC MANGA
品質第一公式商品
STEALING IS EASY - DECIDING
WHAT TO TAKE IS HARD.
VAILABLE NOW AT YOUR FAVORITE
BOOK AND COMIC STORES
T
TEEN
AGE 13+
ng King of Bandits : © 2000 Yuichi Kumakura
www.TOKYOPOP.com

TOKYOPOP®

Is It A Game - Or Is It *Real?*

.hack

// LEGEND OF THE TWILIGHT™

Story by Tatsuya Hamazaki • Art by Rei Izumi

Log On To This Year's Most Exciting Manga!

Available at your favorite book and comic stores

Experience .hack on the PlayStation®2 available from Bandai!

PlayStation 2 .hack INFECTION www.dothack.com

PlayStation 2 .hack MUTATION

PlayStation 2 .hack OUTBREAK

PlayStation 2 .hack QUARANTINE Part 4

© Project .hack 2003. ©2003 TOKYOPOP Inc. All rights reserved. TM&© 2001-2003 Bandai. Program © 2001-2003 Bandai "PlayStation" and the "PS" Family logo are trademarks of Sony Computer Entertainment Inc. The ratings icon is a registered trademark of the Entertainment Software Association.

www.TOKYOPOP.com

Dancing Was Her Life

Her Dance Partner Might Be Her Future

Available Now At Your Favorite Book and Comic Stores

www.TOKYOPOP.com

©Hinako Ashihara

TOKYOPOP®

TOKYOPOP

The most exciting manga release of 2004 is almost here!

T
TEEN
AGE 13+

www.TOKYOPOP.com

©2003 Natsuki Takaya

A WACKY MANGA OF ALIEN FROGS & WORLD DOMINATION
BY MINE YOSHIZAKI

AVAILABLE MARCH 2004
AT YOUR FAVORITE BOOK AND COMIC STORES

SGT. FROG © 1999 MINE YOSHIZAKI. ©2003 TOKYOPOP Inc.

www.TOKYOPOP.com

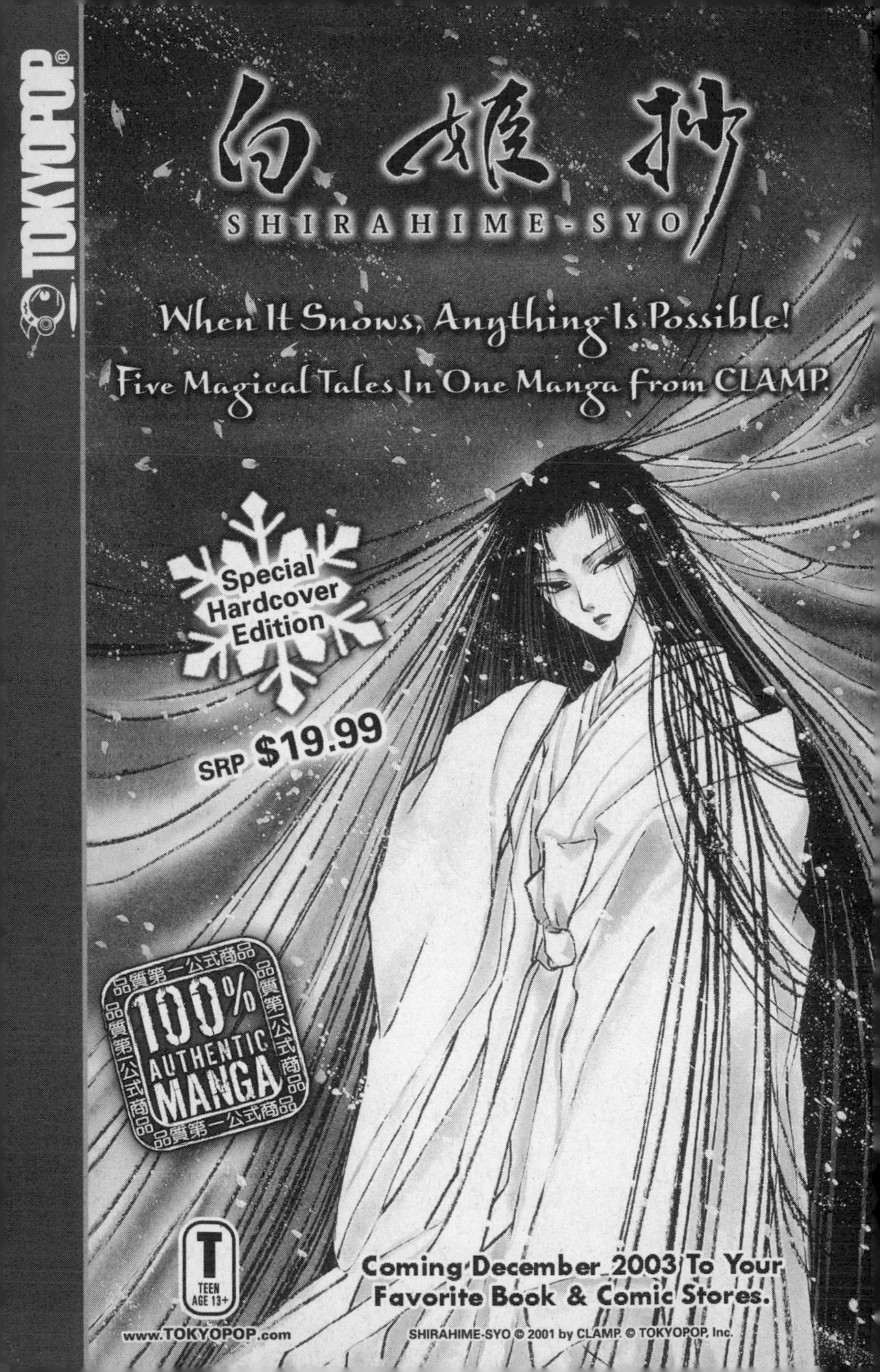
TOKYOPOP
白姫抄
SHIRAHIME-SYO
When It Snows, Anything Is Possible!
Five Magical Tales In One Manga from CLAMP.
Special Hardcover Edition
SRP $19.99
品質第一公式商品
100% AUTHENTIC MANGA
T TEEN AGE 13+
Coming December 2003 To Your Favorite Book & Comic Stores.
www.TOKYOPOP.com
SHIRAHIME-SYO © 2001 by CLAMP. © TOKYOPOP, Inc.

TOKYOPOP
DIGITAL
DIGIMON
MONSTERS
TM
100% AUTHENTIC MANGA
品質第一公式商品
Digivolving Into
Digi - Manga!
Digital Monsters Available Now!
Digimon: Zero Two Coming Soon
To your favorite Book and Comic Stores
A
ALL AGES
www.TOKYOPOP.com
Digimon: TM & © 2002 Akiyoshi Hongo, Toei Animation Co. Ltd.